Dad is a singer.

He sings all day long.

Song, after song,

after song, after song!

He sings to the cat and he sings to the dog.

He sings in the sun

and he sings in the fog.

He sings in the shops

and he sings in the shed.

He sings in the bus

and he sings in his bed.

He sings when he's fishing.

He sings when he jogs.

He sings when he's digging

and chopping up logs.

Mum tells Dad off.
"I'm fed up with that song."

Mum *never* sings . . .

but she *hums* all day long!